On Cigarette Papers

Pam Zinnemann-Hope

Published by Ward Wood Publishing
6 The Drive
Golders Green
London NW11 9SR
www.wardwoodpublishing.co.uk

ISBN: 978-0-9568969-8-8

British Library Cataloguing in Publication Data. A CIP record for this book can be obtained from the British Library.

Designed and typeset in Palatino Linotype by
Ward Wood Publishing
Cover design by Mike Fortune-Wood
Artwork by Peter Davies

Printed and bound in Great Britain by
Imprint Digital, Seychelles Farm,
Upton Pyne, Exeter EX5 5HY

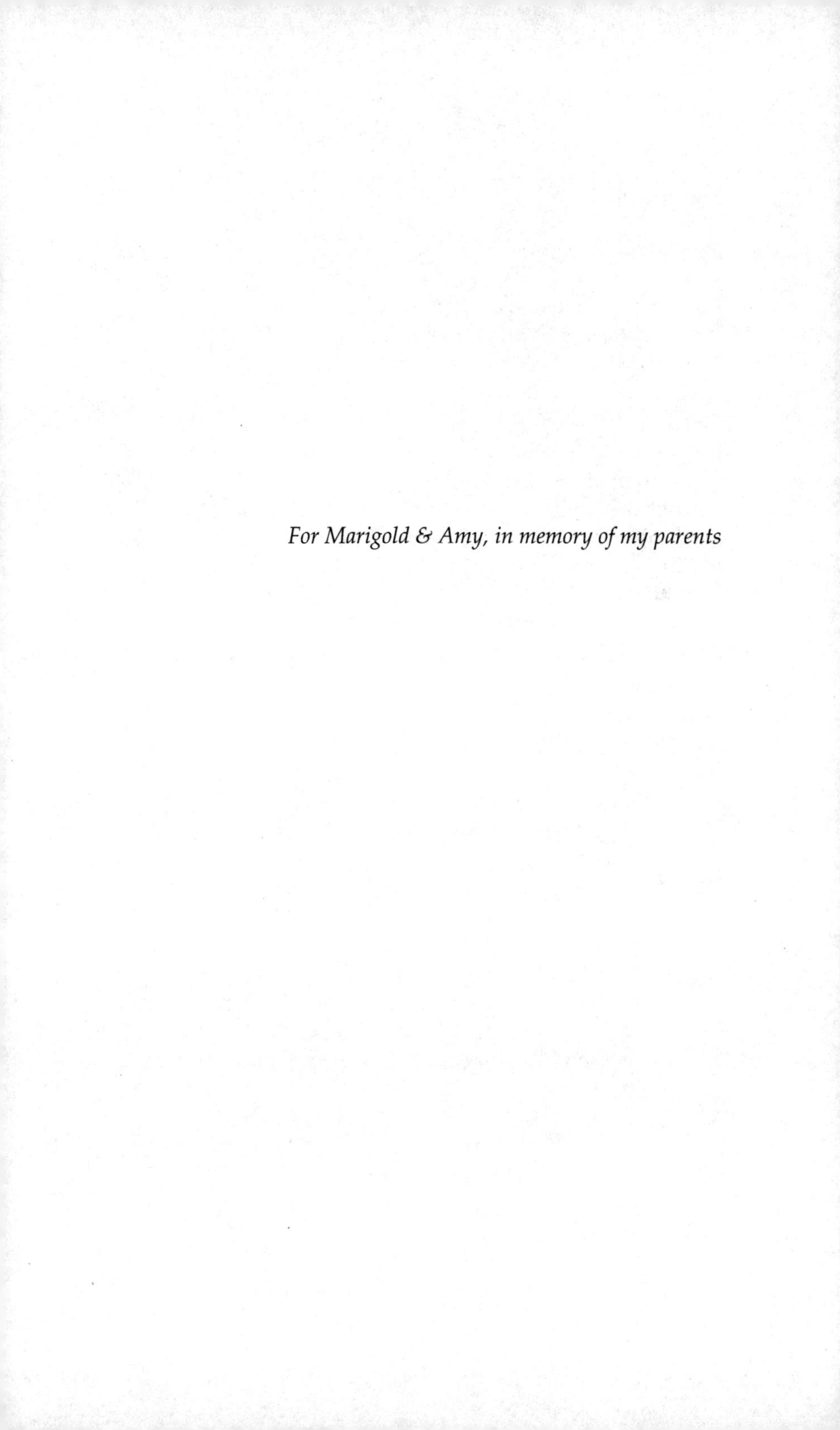

For Marigold & Amy, in memory of my parents

Contents

Arrested

England

Isle Of Man

From Erfurt To Headingley

'The silence that comes out of inarticulateness is the inchoate and desperate silence of chaos. The silence that comes after words is the fullness from which our perceptions can crystallize.'

Eva Hoffman, *Lost in Translation*

Foreword

In 1935 my parents eloped from Hitler's Germany to Kharkov, Ukraine, in the USSR. My mother was German, my father German Jewish. In 1937 they were imprisoned during the Stalin Purges. They were released in 1938 and came to England via Krakow in Poland, where my father had an uncle.

These are the barest bones of a love story lived through some of the worst horrors of 20th century Europe, that my parents could hardly mention when they were alive. They told me that talking about it gave them nightmares but for me their silence meant that I was frequently unable to understand them while I was growing up, and even later on; and I think they often found it difficult to understand me.

When my mother died in 1990, two years after my father, I found an archive of letters, photos and objects that she had left me. Amongst the things in the archive was a tiny pile of cigarette papers with writing pencilled in her hand. Surely these were recipes? I was feeling heartbroken and via the cigarette papers I set out on a journey of discovery through my parents' story and the wider story of my family. I had known all the characters, except for Grossvater Erich, my maternal grandfather and my father's Uncle Marek.

While I was growing up I felt almost as though there were ghosts; things I could sense but that had no names; feelings I wanted to get away from because they were uncomfortable. Being an only child and only grandchild didn't help me, it meant there was no-one to discuss things with. But in 1990 I was also able to go through the archive and to speak with my mother's three remaining friends.

On Cigarette Papers is my version of the truth; a way of holding a conversation with my parents and grandparents about their past – even though they are dead – about its fall-out for them and its implications for me and for my sense of identity. The poems have been conceived between the two languages and cultures I grew up with, English and German, but the story of my family is also shaped by a third language that I don't speak: Russian, the language of the cigarette papers.

Dramatis Personae

Myself, born 1945

My Mother, Lottie, born 1911

My Father, Kurt, born 1906

Grossvater Erich, born 1880 } my German maternal
Grossma Hertha, born 1890 } grandparents

Opa Lazar, born 1875 } my Jewish paternal
Oma Leah, born 1885 } grandparents

Uncle Marek, my father's uncle & Oma Leah's brother. He died in Auschwitz

Evelyn, my mother's help

Erna, a German communist friend of my parents, married to another German Communist

Prologue: Headingley 1990

My Translations From The Mysterium

In the library where the carved mice
lie in wait on each oak chair,
I'm trying to understand how the cold front
leaks down over me from the forests of Pomerania.
I'm trying to make translations
from the Mysterium...

Wenn man in den Eiszapfen schaut

If you look into the icicle,
into the transparent world of its ice
and the water melting on its surface,
perhaps you can see a story

Der Winter ist eisig kalt.
Der Schnee liegt vielleicht hübsch auf dem Grund,
aber das Herz der Menschen ist gefroren

The winter is ice-cold.
The snow may look beautiful underfoot
but the heart of the people is frozen;
even my beaver lamb jacket
cannot keep mine warm...

What's the use of translation?

...Why am I here on this hill?
They think I'm still on the train.
I can hold down my hat
and cling to the fence;
the wind beating me in the dark
knows I'm here
and all this white stuff coming down.
It keeps coming down.

The Attic

In the attic
I find my mother has left
her two black fabric travelling bags,

with the exact space between them for her
slightly bending her knees
as she lets go the handles.

*

I find
fifty pencilled recipes,
on cigarette papers, in Russian.

And I wonder, did my mother
collect one from each woman
in her prison?

What were their names,
what dish did each dream?
Kiev, nineteen thirty-seven.

*

There are sacks of wool
piled up in the garden now, mother.
In my recurring dream

I come home alone;
strange men are stacking up the sacks,
barring the way to the door.

I ask for you
and no one knows
the house belongs to us.

Germany 1933-5

Frankfurt, 1933

My Mother's Courtship

As his assistant,
I help him
with his research in microbiology

until he leaves flowers for me,
violets and snowdrops,
in the wrong hat in the vestibule.

A blond Aryan is my decoy,
he bets me I'll never marry a Jew;
he still owes me.

When I keep rendez-vous with him
im Stadtwald beim Forsthaus,
we arrive separately...

...Every relationship is a shared secret.

Im Stadtwald beim Forsthaus – In the town wood, near the Forsthaus, the Ranger's House, a well-known café at the time

My Mother Signs 'Heil Hitler'

It's 1933.
At work a circular comes round
asking everyone from now on
to sign every letter
with 'Heil Hitler!'

To agree you have to sign a chit.

I sign. I shouldn't have.
But then if I had not,
what good
would it have done?

Oma Leah Hears The News

When Kurt and Lottie tell me that they'll marry
I fall to my knees immediately,

I beg you, please don't choose my son, Lottie,
I want him to live with me.

Of course I would prefer if you were Jewish!

Frankfurt a.Main. Den 3.4.1933

Der Magistrat – Personaldezernent

Herrn
Dr. Kurt Zinnemann
d.d. Stadtsgesundheitsamt

In view of the necessity to reduce staffing costs
we herewith terminate your employment
on thirtieth April, nineteen thirty three,
in accordance with Part Four, Chapter One,
Paragraph One, Section Two
of the Prussian Savings Decree, dated
Twelfth, O Nine, nineteen thirty;
but reserve the right to authorize immediate dismissal
in case of appropriate legal authorisation.

Acknowledgement of Receipt required!

Der Magistrat - Personaldezernent –
Borough Council - Human Resources
Stadtgesundheitsamt – City Health Authority

My Father Tells About 1934

I'm working in the Jewish Hospital now,
walk out onto the street;
someone comes up to me rattling a tin
collecting for the Nazis.

I tell her, You should be ashamed of yourself,
collecting for such a cause.

From out of my words, around a corner,
four SS appear to arrest me.

I feel a pause; a crowd of ordinary
Frankfurt people form around me,
move forward spontaneously,
push me into a tram.

Father, do you hate the Germans?

I owe my life to them.

Grossvater Erich Reacts

Lottie! Ich seh Dich lieber
auf dem Friedhof liegen
als mit diesem Juden leben!

Lottie! I prefer to see you
in a grave,
than married
to a Jew!

en route,1934

My Mother's Bowls

It's December the first. Good-bye Frankfurt.
We won't shop for *Stollen* at the *Weihnachtsmarkt.*
But I've brought the recipe. I remembered.

My pyrex bowls packed carefully in my suitcase;
Kurt's large grey valise with his initials.
His parents are riding in the train a little way with us.

I feel as though a block of ice
chills the walls of my stomach.

I ask his mother,
Can I call you Mother now?

Ein Löfel schmalz
Vanille, Zitronen,
Fünfundzwanzig gramm Hefe

Oma Leah's Lament

They're travelling far away.
It's fertile, though desolate, the Ukraine.

They're leaving me alone
with the man I was forced to marry.

My son will celebrate
a secular wedding.

This young shiksa tells me she loves him.
She can never love him like me.

Grossvater Erich Makes A Phone Call

Guten Tag, Herr Göring.
Hier spricht Major Loesch.
Wie geht es Ihnen?

Good afternoon Herr Göring.
Major Loesch here.
How are you?

A young Jew
is eloping.
He's on the train
going East
to Russia, with my daughter.

Could you close
the border please...

Grossma Chants

If they find them
It'll all be over:
Kurt'll be taken.
Lottie'll be broken.

I can't save her.

If they find them
He'll not forgive her.
Lottie'll be bitter.
They'll both be broken.

I can't save him.

They mustn't find her
With her Jewish lover.
The truth is bitter.
My heart is broken.

I can't save her.

Russia

Headingley,1965

My Mother Behind Glass

I'm standing by the window with you,
the way I've always done.
We're looking out. There's someone
standing in the fresh snow
on the frozen lake. I think it's me,
wrapped up warm against the creeping cold
in my grey tweed coat and scarf,
my gloves and hat.

And yet here I stand with you
inside the window with the net curtain
looking out, the way we've always done,
at me standing out there.

Chebureks
Saloniki phalava
Oroshka
Varyeniki
Kulebyaka

Poland, December 1934

My Mother Waits In Krakow Station

A Polish lord
pale-skinned, chin up
sweeps down the staircase
in his floor-length fur and hat;
no scruples he has in his village
at using his *droit du seigneur,*
I'm sure.

Frankfurt, December 1934

Grossma's Letter

The smell of baking drifting from the kitchen.
My coffee. My cigarette smoke curls
into the Gobelin curtains,
into the pink fabrics of the salon.

It's December.
And I'm perched in my elbow chair.
I take it out of my shirt,
the letter. It's from Lottie.

They're in Poland. They're going to Russia.
They've got jobs there. They're going to marry,
Lottie and Kurt, her Jew.
They're staying in Krakow. With his Jewish uncle.

This is madness.
My feet on the thick green carpet.
What can I do? How shall I manage?
He mustn't know, my husband.

Here, in my bedroom,
in my jewel box with gold deco inlay
and little drawers that swivel outwards,
I turn the key.
In the bottom, there!
That's where I hide it.

She isn't here.
She won't be here for Christmas.

I'm stroking my blonde hair with the brush,
watching myself in the mirror:
I will continue to manicure my nails,
to file them to their sharp points,
I say to myself;
I will continue to dress well.
I will continue to visit my mother.
Nothing is altered.

What My Father Tells My Mother On The Train To Russia

That line of geese is stitching the sky with invisible words,
words I'll whisper in your ear tonight as the train travels
east;
east, where the geese are slowly descending to snow;
snow. Look, quick! How their breasts fall like blood.
Blood, they say, is thicker than water – not mine;
you're mine, love, I fit with you, as hand does to glove.
Glove.

My Mother Waits In Kharkov Station, USSR

I look up the steps to the lavatory
to see a peasant woman
– stall door open –
in headscarf and bright patterned dress;
she squats on the seat
like over a hole in the ground,
her breath steaming.

Kharkov, Winter 1935

My Mother Tells Me About Learning Russian

I only know German.
At first manage with gestures and guessing.

Then I go to lectures,
let the sea of sounds wash into me,
listen to the radio,
to the deep music and the tiny
insistent lappings of the language
until words are landed in my ear.

Potschemu – Why?

The scientific words, like *algebra,* are similar.
Not so *krasnia* – red, *krasivi* – beautiful;
nor *zolutu* – gold,
the gold cupola on Saint Sophia;
inside, the incense rises secretly towards heaven.

My dreams begin to come in Russian, eventually.
Russians are keen on dreams.

(But in the Kiev prison mine fade.
I tread a fine line there
between language and reality;
interrogated – I keep silent.)

babka
chebureks
saloniki pahlava
charlotte pelmeni
vareniks

Thirty-Five Degrees of Frost

His Snapshot of Me

In the park,
in Kharkov,
in a small fur hat
and muff,
a long fur coat and boots,
in the snow
with mystery tracks
and long thin shadows,
all the birch trees
standing bare
behind me.
He takes my photo.

My Snapshot of Him

Look at him;
his double-breasted coat,
his tall fur hat –
imposing –
my handsome researcher.

Frankfurt, 1935

Grossvater Erich Hums While He Washes His Hands

Ich kaufte meiner Tochter,
meiner Puppe,
zu jeder Saison einen Mantel.

Jetzt braucht sie noch einen wärmeren.
In ihrem weit entfernten Leben
lass sie frieren!

I bought my daughter, my doll,
a coat for every season.

Now she needs
a warmer coat.

In her distant life,
let her freeze.

Kharkov, February 7th 1935

My Mother Describes Her Wedding Party

Because bureaucrats
muddle the date
we have our wedding party,
a few Russian friends,
seven days early:

we have caviar
at our party.

*

February 14th

Her Wedding Day

No ceremony in Russia then:
we get a slip of paper
through a *guichet,*
go back to work.

Solyanka
Pilaff
Paskha
Pavlova
Mazzurka

Kharkov 1936

My Father Reads The Brochure For A Putyovka To My Mother

Visit the sea, and take the Crimean sun!
Citizens of the USSR, you have a right to recreation!
The Moorish style castles
and exquisite country houses,
once out of your price range,
have now become state property – sanatoria,
designed and arranged for *your* needs.
We offer special diets, under medical supervision,
a dancing master from Moscow,
organized visits to the region.
A Crimean putyovka!
Apply for it as a bonus.

Putyovka – literally 'a journey', in fact a holiday

Ghurzuff, Crimea, May 1937

My Father Writes A Postcard To His Friend Franz Gugenheim

I'm writing from the terrace overlooking the park
to tell you what the sanatorium's house rules are:

treatment on arrival to kill lice and flees;
no smoking in the building;
no alcoholic drinks in- or outside the premises;
lights out by eleven,
men and women in separate rooms;
instant expulsion if disobedience looms!

But as usual in Russia,
there's a way round these rules…

Smetana
Schi
chebureks
vareniks

My Father Sings A Love Song To My Mother in the Bay of Ghurzuff

I took my lover to a mountain,
the air was warm at first and clear,
the morning sky like blue hibiscus
as we climbed above the pines.

With a bribe of wine and vodka
to the man who fetched the ice
I took my Lottie in his open lorry,
north side of the Yaila Peaks.

On a bend our Tatar driver,
with blue hibiscus in his turban,
oversteered, and in that moment
a back wheel spun off the edge.

Below us, the sea, like blue hibiscus,
the sand, too hot to touch;
in a hidden crevasse above us,
the snow on the Yaila Mountains.

That night I gave my love a polka,
on our *putyovka* she danced the *hopak*
in her dress like blue hibiscus;
her poise like the 'swallows nest' castle perched on the rock.

We drank a red Kamin Alushta;
we learnt the rhythms of the *mazurka.*
Today I gave my lover two thousand roses
from the Nikitsky Gardens, a mountain of roses.

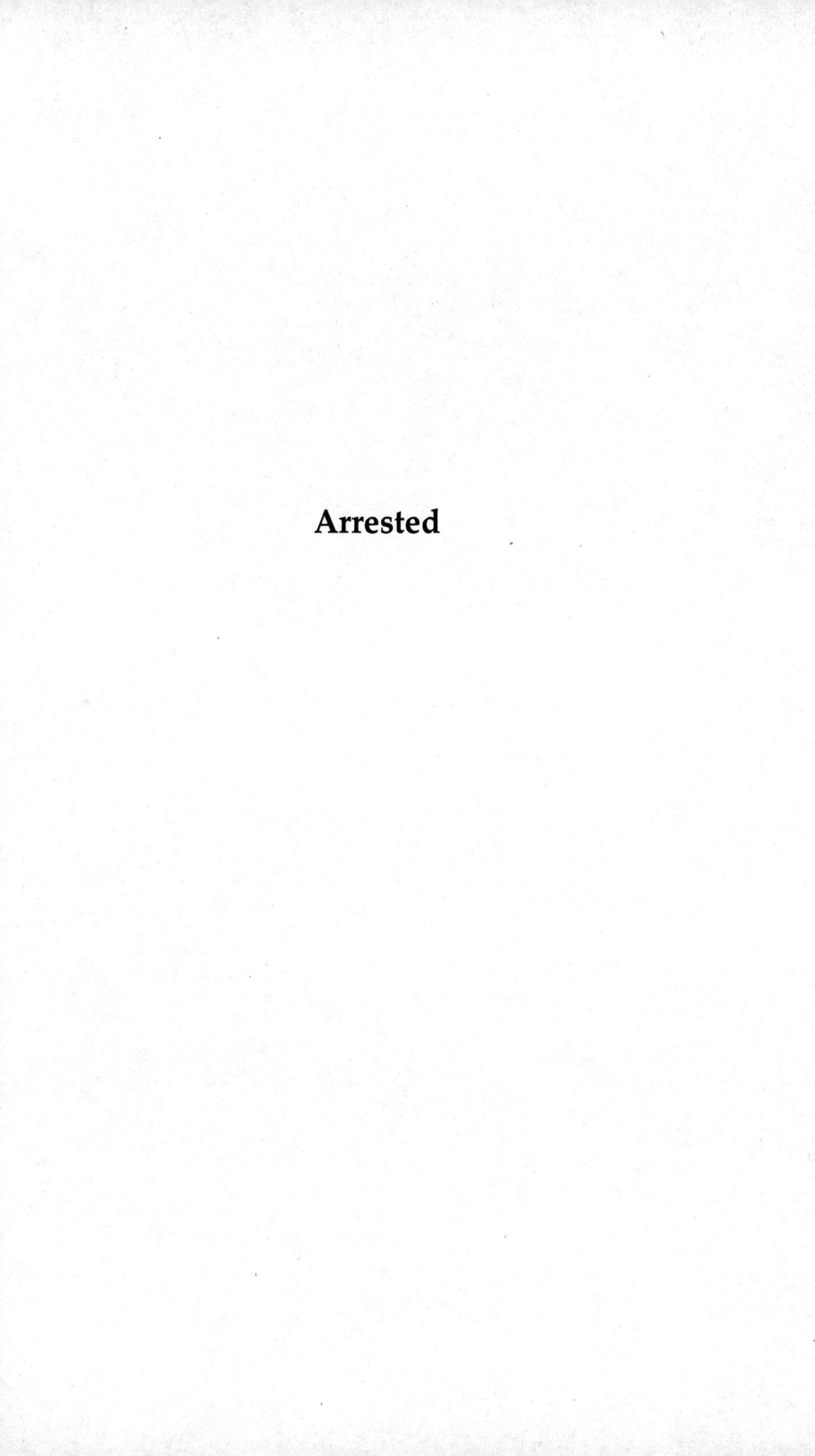

Arrested

Kharkov, August 1937

Arrest

Every night we lie awake
sweating in the August heat.
One night: 4.00am,
Kurt says,
'Listen!'
A muffled engine sound;
the quiet click:
the van doors shutting
before it comes, the dreaded,
half-expected knock.

I find us some clothes
and see the van
known as Black Crow
from the window;
and the Crow's disguise:
letters denoting 'Meat Van'
everyone can recognize.

They take us down together.
I have no time to say 'good-bye'.
I watch his straight back bend
as they shove him in;
I see how he bows his head
before they push me too.

There is no time to say good-bye.

Kharkov, August 1937

Erna's Tale

How come my husband is arrested
for 'crimes against the State'?

I need to find comfort.
I want to see my friends.
I set off for Kurt and Lottie's in the heat.

Their landlady doesn't speak,
she points at their boarded-up door.

Frankfurt, January 1938

Grossma's Letters

Liebe Mutti,
Ich bin sehr glücklich....

Hier ist ihr letzter Brief.

Er kam in einem braunen Kuvert
von Russland,
in spitzer Schrift, wie immer,
damit man nicht weiss
von wem er ist.

Alle Briefe liegen in meinem Schmuckkästchen
von meinem Mann versteckt.
Er glaubt, sie hat mir nie geschrieben.

Es werden jetzt sechs Monate.
Ich warte jeden Tag.
Kein Wort von ihr.
Und ich kann es ihm nicht einmal erzählen.

Dear Mother,
I'm very happy....

This is her last letter.

It came in a brown envelope
from Russia,
in spiky writing, as usual,
so you can't tell who it's from.

All her letters lie in my jewel box
hidden from my husband.
He believes she's never written…

It's been six months now.
Not a word from her.
And I can't even tell him.

Leeds, 1990

On Cigarette Papers

(My Interpretation)

'Russische Kochrezepte, nicht wegwerfen',
Russian recipes, don't throw away;
I tip them out of their small envelope,

wonder who saved the papers,
where she found the pencil
since writing was forbidden;

the flimsy pile sits soft
in my palm, till I hand them over.
Each edge is foxed.

*

The translator is trying to decipher
the Russian through a reading glass;
she might smudge the rhythms

of my mother's hand as she shuffles
the fifty slips, turns some over to scan
the writing on the reverse...

She tells me, 'here's *kvass,*
a national drink, illegible
at the end; lemon jam, unfinished;

twice *kulebyaka,* both incomplete;
varyeniki, lazybones curd parcels,
with half the method, served with butter, sprinkled with
sugar...'

*

In the cramped space
on the stone floor
my mother and her

cell-mates live on
black bread and cabbage;
they call up

the normal kitchen chat,
the swapping of recipes
out of their cavernous hunger,

making feasts.
In her neat Cyrillic
my mother is noting

a dish from each woman,
practicing the language
to hold her mind.

*

'Your mother's notes are misspelt,
her verbs – infinitives,
hurried, furtive...'

I think my mother hopes
she might get out, be in
a kitchen, gather ingredients:

here's food from Latvia,
Georgia, Greece, Ukraine, Russia,
Jewish herring, fish in aspic...

her lists on cigarette papers;
my only map
of who is with her.

Kiev Prison, 1937

My Mother Tells About Her Washbag

We have to cross
a cold stone courtyard
with our washbags;
we have to walk naked
while male guards
watch us.
I feel covered in bedbugs.

Recipe No. 36

Apples
?
Apple
?
Panful of water
600 grammes sugar
serve chilled

My Mother Tells About The Cubicles

One day I'm
taken for interrogation.
Kept, as usual, in a cubicle to wait:

in the cubicle
the roof is so low
you can't stand up
you can't sit
the seat is so narrow.

I tap on the wooden wall
to the left, to ask,
Hello. Who's there?
The answer comes slowly.
Good. Not a stool pigeon then,
– he'd be too quick at the code.

'Who is with you in your cell?'
I tap him all our names
– a hundred and ten women
in a cell for twenty-five.
He taps me all the names in his
and more. 'Some have been moved on,
or shot. Who knows?'
Have you heard of Kurt Zinnemann?
The answer comes,
'No.'

I have a tiny pencil stub
wound illegally under my hair.
I pull it out:

Kurt, I love you,
Lottie.

I scratch it on the door.

Recipe No. 38

Boulki
Two hours of dough
It has to rise
It has to be - not hard
Then give it a shape
Paint it with yolk
Pour sugar over it
And vanilla butter.

My Mother Tells…

Days later,
by chance,
I'm thrown into
that cubicle again,
to find –

Lottie, I love you,
Kurt.

My Mother Dreams

I can almost remember
the feel of my green linen table cloth;
flowers,
a little honeysuckle perhaps,
a *Rose à Parfum de Bulgarie;*
make it a bouquet
and a little cut glass vase to put it in
and place it in the centre of the table with the green linen
table cloth.
Let my cloth have embroidery.
Give me the smell of frying onions, please,
and the sight of the steam rising
– like wraiths from the broth.
Let the broth be thick,
let it come out of a tureen
so full that whatever I eat it can't be emptied
and let the rolls be white and light
and covered with poppyseed and served with butter.

And let the next course come.
Let it be schnitzel in pastry,
Crimean aubergines, potato pie.
And for dessert I'll pipe white heaps onto rice paper,
bake them at a hundred and thirty;
I'll serve meringues on a plate of blue sky.

en route May, 1938

Release

I

My Mother Tells About Leaving Russia

The wheels clank their slow way;
the couplings are whistling
the same two flat notes.

My underwear, my fur coat,
my hat and my rings –
is all they gave me.

Your father
with his shaven head
sits upright beside me

starved
and deprived of sleep
for two weeks.

I confessed to nothing
because, he says,
your life depended on me.

The couplings still whistle
the same two flat notes.
The train pushes us over

the Polish border –
like one flesh – we get up
and step off.

I, swollen
from malnutrition,
in my furs,

your father, thin,
thin, in a suit.
An elegant couple!

II

My Father Tells About The Polish Border

We are given tickets to Berlin
- compliments of the Führer -
and money for one day's food.

A ride to Berlin
is a ticket to death,
for a Jew that's married a German.

Nazis (or not)
the Red Cross trade money
for your mother's gold rings .

III

My Father Tells About Warsaw

Another train. A change of gauge.
A different destination.

I take a chance,
ask the German Consul,

Please can you lend me forty dollars?
My father in Frankfurt will repay it.

This man, knowing, shakes my hand
– the hand of a Jew –

gives me the money,

Ich wünsche Ihnen Glück,
I wish you luck.

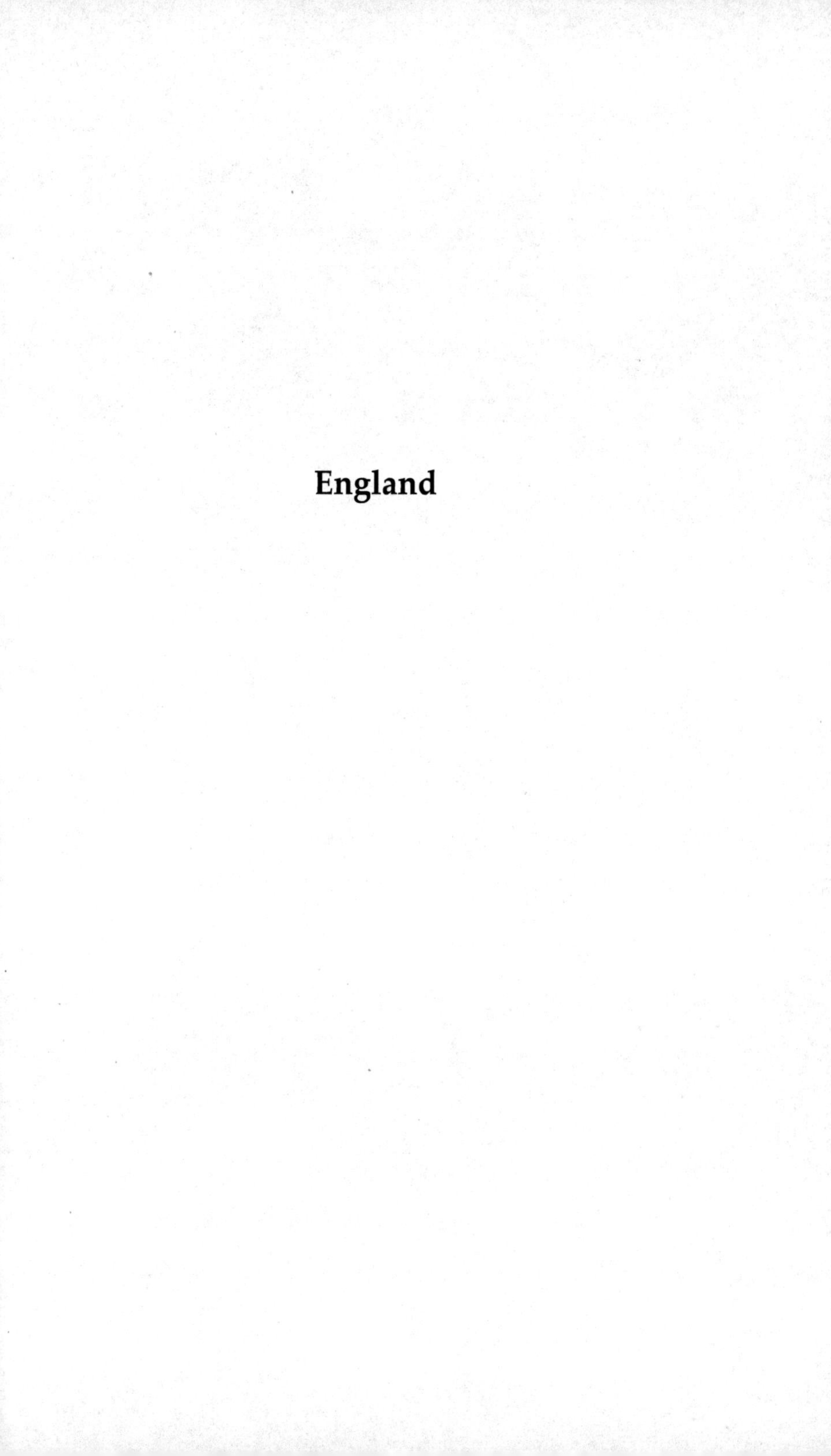

England

Frankfurt, May/June1938

Grossma Gets Word

Poststempel London.
Was für ein Brief ist das?
Was sagt es hier,
die Schrift so wackelig:
'Endlich gut ernährt, und...'
Keine Unterschrift,
eine anscheinende Geheimschrift,
das ist ja von der Lottie.
Sie ist in einem normalen Land,
Gott sei Dank!
Und was für eine Angst!

The postmark says London.
What sort of letter is this?
And what does it say here?
The writing's so wobbly:
'We're well fed at last
and ...'
No signature, it's like a code.
This letter's from Lottie.
She's reached a normal country.
Thank God!

All that fear...!

Cockfosters, May/June 1938
c/o Dr Franz Gugenheim

My Father Writes to Uncle Marek

Lieber Onkel Marek,

Thank you for taking us in after Kiev,
for keeping us,
in spite of the imminent danger
from the Nazis.
– No. I'd better cross that out
I don't know who might read it! –
Till Franz's parents could buy us our tickets
from Danzig.
And thank you for the beautiful clothes you bought us.
I hope all is well with you, as it is with us now,
here at Franz's.

As we sailed towards England through the Kiel Canal
we saw grass so green, it almost hurt.
And a line of cows a short way off,
who looked, to us, almost like magical beasts.
Strange. It wasn't milking time,
there was no farmer in sight,
but they were facing, as it were,
an invisible conductor,
the way a choir would if cows could sing;
and I began to wonder
what their song would be:
would they sing about juicy flavours of grass,
of buttercup heaven that comes only in May?
Perhaps – from a race memory – they'd sing
of how they once roamed wild in herds;
of being chased by wolves.
What would they sing about being confined to fields?

My Father Gets A Break

From Kharkov I corresponded with
Prof McLeod from Leeds.

In June, at last, he learns our fate
via the Refugee Committee.

He sends me the offer of a job.
The day of the interview I oversleep.

Franz has to jump up and drive me to King's Cross
against the clock, in his pyjamas.

Virginia Road To Grove Lane

My Mother Tells Of Settling

First a flat in Virginia Road.
Then our house
in Grove Lane, Headingley:
it becomes a kind of root.

And yet,
I sit and twiddle
the radio knobs;
I find myself
searching for a Russian station.

*

My Father At Home

Here in England
I'll grow English roses
for you, Lottie,
in our own garden.
The frequent rain will help.

*

My Mother At Home

Tonight I'll bake my Kurt an apple
an English cooking apple;
I'll fill it up with spices,
encase it in sweet pastry
to make it rich and good;
I'll bake my love an English pud.

Drunken Cherry – Torte
That the dough should not be very hard,
take out the cherries from the liquid.
To leave a little bit of dough
and to grate this bit and just cover
the top with this

Frankfurt, 1939

Oma Leah Talks To Opa Lazar About Leaving

My son.
My son Kurt.
My son the doctor.
He earns too little money as a refugee.
But he's helping us go to England.
Only just in time!
He's a good boy,
a real Mensch.
He's arranged a guarantor for us,
a doctor Mau-rice Gor-don, in Leeds,
even though he can't support us;
even though his wife's a goy.

Headingley, April 1939

Oma Leah Arrives In England with Opa Lazar

You know our Etam sign was trampled underfoot;
they took silk stockings and lace panties for their girls;

they smashed our window in the *Kaiserstrasse;*
I daren't go out, just sat at home and cried.

Werner May brought us bread and sausage on his bike
each day. And when Kurt's letter came,

with our guarantor's name, (to get us out to England),
I didn't think to gather up our family photos –

just shoved some silver in my handbag:
the Pesach cup, the little dish, the best salt-cellar,

the tiny locket and my gold ring set with Kurt's milk teeth;
I added in my tiny diamond earrings – I'd hidden them all –

and then, so nobody could touch my precious *Schmuck,*
I filled my bag to the brim with pins and needles –

Feel them, Lottie, feel them!

Schmuck – jewellery

Isle Of Man

Headingley, September 1939

My Mother's Declaration

A child in my belly. That would be good.
I'd like to have your child at last.

Now war's declared, how long will it last?
A child born in wartime would not be good.

We felt that coming here was good.
We thought the peace would never last.

A child of ours must be safe, at last.
It will bring us hope. Let's wait, be good.

Headingley, May 17th 1940

My Mother Revisits His Arrest

I try to forget how it comes,
the unexpected knock. The police.

We're classified Category C, I say.

'Enemy Aliens; Not Dangerous,' he says,
'I know. I'm sorry, Madam.
Sir, you'll have to come with me.'

Kurt packs his shaving kit and brush.
Hardly time to say good-bye.

Outside I hear a blackbird sing.
This time, I know, it won't be long.

Letters

Central Promenade Camp, Douglas,
Isle of Man, May 17th 1940

Dearest Lottie,
First of all, I am alright. Do not quit
the house. If the war goes well
we shall be there together.
If not, we may never see each other.
However it works out, be always
as brave and good as you have been, my dear.
My deepest love, Kurt

May 23rd

Lottie Dearest,
I need an operation for my tonsils
but the doctor cannot allow it.
I will manage.
Kiss and love, ever yours, Kurt

May 24th

Dearest,
Two hundred medics in my camp, mostly specialists!
We sleep two to a bed.
Still no letter from you…

Grove Lane, Headingley, May 25th

Kurt Darling,
You may have heard,
I have to go as well.
Do not worry about me,
there was worse behind us.
All my love, Lottie.

L. Zinnemann,
c/o Mrs Harrison,
Beechburn House,
Ballafasson Rd,
Port Erin,
Isle of Man

May 26th

We women, mostly Jews,
some Germans like me,
jeered at in Liverpool...

May 27th

I hoped to have a letter from you to-day.
So far I've not had any.
I dreamt the grant from the university came
to thirty-six pounds a year and you couldn't manage.
I hope this letter will reach you,
somehow.
All my love Dearest

*

June 4th
'Opened by Censor 2674'

Kurt, Darling,
That is the fifth letter I've written
since I was taken.
I don't know whether any reached you,
or whether you have written?
Nothing has come.
I want to know how you are...
Potschemu?
Why you?
Why me?
All my love, Lottie

June 5th

Still I hear nothing .
Lottie Dearest, I want to hold you.

This captivity lets me wander free;
I cook, yet feel eaten up;
have books, but cannot concentrate;
swim, though the water is cold;
all I can think of
is our release.
When will it be?

Lottie,
Your first letters arrived

Darling Kurt,
I've heard nothing from you again

My dearest Lottie
Sensation of today –
the arrival of father…

*

August 10th

Leah,
Every day, swimming in the sea.
Kurt does my washing.
Our son the doctor,
he gave a lecture,
went well, I heard.
The scientists amuse themselves,
hearing each other and learning.
The musicians, they give concerts,
rehearse for a Camp Review.
Me, I take the sun, with my son!
Yours Lazar

*

September 21st

Dearest,.........Father cannot be released
before November, when he's sixty-five...

Douglas, August

The Ballad Of The German Refugee

Am Pfingstsonntag, im strahlenden Morgenschein
Nach des Frühstücks bescheidenem Schmaus,
Fanden sich zwei sehr freundliche Herrn bei mir ein,
Mit dem Auto bereit vor dem Haus.
Und im Rathaus, da traf ich noch andere dann,
Die so freundlich geholt worden warn,
Und dort sagte uns ein viel höherer Mann
Dass wir bald über Land sollten fahrn.

Das ist die Ballad' vom Deutschen Refugee,
Wer sie nicht erlebt hat, der begreift sie nie.

On Whit Sunday, in the early sun's rays,
After breakfast, that modest little feast,
Two friendly men appeared at my place
With their car outside my house, like the police.
In the Town Hall, where I met others like me
Who'd been fetched by the same friendly band,
We were told by a definitely senior man,
Be prepared! You'll go travelling overland.

This is the ballad of the German Refugee.
If you've not lived it, you'll not understand,
forgive me!

'The Ballad of the German Refugee' was written for a camp revue which took place during the summer of 1940. It was a handout for a sing-a-long.

Port Erin, November 1941

My Mother Knits

On the Isle of Man I'm knitting him a tie,
a dark brown tie. With each stitch
I pull the wool across my heart.

All night I think I see the war planes overhead.
We aren't allowed to listen to the news
or read the papers, in case we might be spies;

but for his birthday I'm knitting him a tie.
Each stitch is neat and tight.
With each stitch I pull the wool across my heart.

On the day they let the ladies visit Douglas
I take it to him as his present, on the bus,
wondering how he'll be. And there he is,

the first man climbing the gates,
waving at me from the top
and shouting, 'Lottie'.

I feel my Prussian blood run to my face,
and think, 'How undignified my husband is.'

To The Housefather, House Number 6

Punctually at...*three forty-five pm*...hours
on...Monday...*third...second...forty-one...*
the undermentioned internees:-
ZINNEMANN. Kurt
must be at the North Gate of Camp
with their luggage which they will deposit
overnight in the archway passage
at rear of Main Guard room,
where such luggage will be searched
in the presence of the Orderly Officer.

Punctually at...*seven am...*
on *Tuesday fourth...second...forty one...*
these internees
will be at the South gate of Camp
with their three
blankets and a certificate from you
that they have delivered up
all Government property.
If they attempt to carry with them...

on board, February 1941

On The Ferry

Our ferry, the Rushen Castle,
pulls out from Douglas in this gale.
Kurt turns green with her listing.

My beautiful Lottie is pale and drawn.
We cannot dock at Liverpool because of bombing.
We pass the Wyre Light.

Snow over Fleetwood.

From the approach channel
the upper and lower lighthouses are aligned.
They tell us, we're almost in safe harbour.

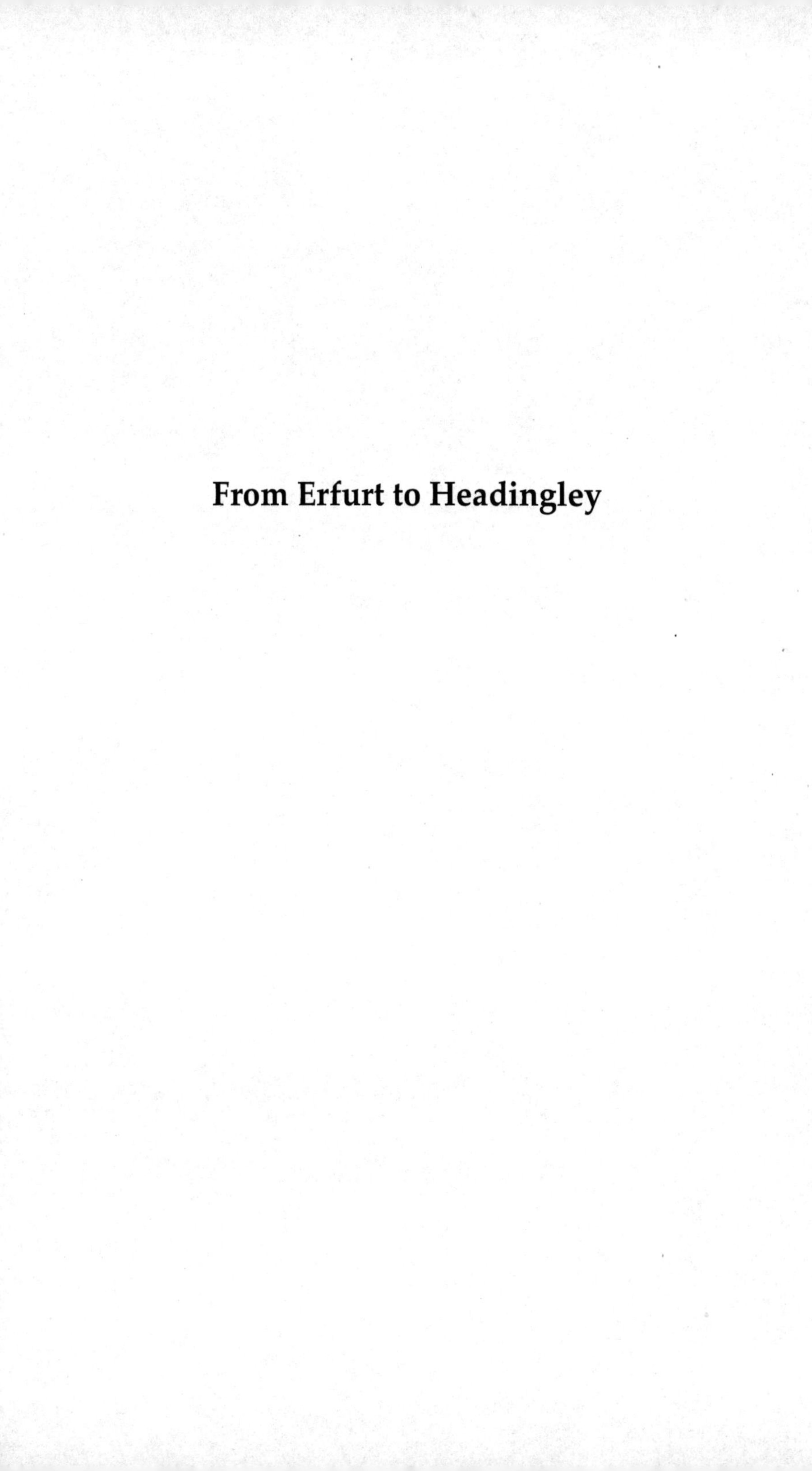

From Erfurt to Headingley

Erfurt, 1947

Grossma Remembers Being At Table With Grossvater Erich In Frankfurt

Wir setzen uns gerade zum Essen
und er ruft das Mädchen zum Tisch,
Alice! Holen Sie bitte die Leiter.
Die Leiter. Ja.
Nun steigen Sie hinauf
bis ganz oben hin.
Schauen Sie jetzt auf den Tisch
und sagen Sie mir, was fehlt.

O ja, sagt Alice. Die Butter.

We're sitting down to eat;
he calls the maid to the table.
Alice! Please fetch the ladder.
Yes, the ladder.
Now, climb up,
right up to the top.
Take a look at the table
and tell me what you forgot.

Oh, says Alice. The butter.

Headingley,1946

Every Night In Her Sleep

(My mother's dream)

It draws me down.
Deep under turquoise
the water is lapping me.

It keeps retreating.

I can feel the yelling
lodged in my chest.
I open my mouth:

no sound comes out.

I try to push it out.
I get no breath.

And it keeps coming back.

Day after day I grasp
at straws of sunlight; I'm
beached on hot dry sand.

Night after night I swim
and stand in this stifling sea.

I want to breathe.

I can feel the silkiness
of the water.
I can open my mouth.

I want to yell.

My face is bursting,
held in by the water,
the power of the water.

And it keeps returning.

Erfurt, 1947

Translation Of A Letter From Grossvater Erich, To My Mother

Nimmer mehr, nimmer mehr.
Im Wald in Bulgarien
schoss ich einmal ein Reh:
Das war in früheren Zeiten.

I shot a deer
in the forest in Bulgaria,
that was in another era.

Dare I dream of the days
when I had cigarettes, salmon, wine and brandy,
the walls weren't perforated by shrapnel,
the windows weren't shattered;
a time before the green carpet was stained
with the jam that kept dropping
off my bread, every night as I walked up and down,

als ich nicht hustete

when I didn't cough,
when you were here.

When you were here
I took you to the Bulgarian forests.
That's where my memories gather
they gather mushrooms;
they gather some for me and some for you.
I've sorted them carefully, the edible from the poisonous
and a pile for the don't know.

You sent me medicines after you ran away.
You are my daughter;
it's been thirteen years since I heard from you.

I sit here coughing,
staring at piles of forest mushrooms.
Shall I leave you some

im Zimmer hier?

in this room?

When shall I see you?

Nimmer mehr.

Nimmer mehr – Never more

Headingley, 1974

The Night Before I Marry

The wine her Nazi father destined for her wedding,
two bottles of white (or maybe a case),
she opens at last, the night before mine
in the Louis Quinze dining-room that came from Erfurt.

We can't drink the soured wine.

Headingley, 1990

My Lost Poem

And now it's gone.
As if it doesn't want to be remembered.
As if I've begun to try to catch
things that don't want to be caught.
This week,
when I was lost
on a hillside with the dog,
trying to figure out my way,
a red deer leaped out of the earth,
the thicket just below me.
Terracotta.
With a crashing of twigs
it alerted me
as it hurled itself into the air,
legs bent for flight
and into the bushes;
it was gone.

Frankfurt, Fichardstr. 11, 10.4.1950

Grossma Writes…

Meine liebe Lottie, mein lieber Kurt,

I've done it!
You'll have seen from my telegram,
I arrived here on Friday.

I crossed the unguarded stretch of border from East to West
illegally, which only cost me twenty-five Ostmark
and a tin of coffee.

I went with a young woman,
we ran up a steep slope
over a wet, ploughed field; it was pitch

black and I thought I wouldn't make it
but the young woman
took my hand and pulled me along…

I am worried about the expense for you
of shipping your furniture,
and it bothers me that I couldn't pay for it…

And I feel dreadful about something else:
I had completely relied on my help
washing the light green carpet with soapy water,

once she'd beaten it,
which she did say she would do,
and I never checked;

while things were being packed
into the chests I saw, to my horror,
that no cleaning had taken place;

I am so sorry. It leaves me
no peace.
Before your Papa died

he often walked around at night
with bread and honey or bread and jam
and caused the stains with his pipe…

Now the past time seems like a bad dream…
Everything is still whirling around, my dear ones.
Give little Pamela a kiss.

Headingley, 1950

My Mother Waits For The Furniture

My dreams of Bauhaus furniture,
that slick, sleek, contemporary look,
bow out.

No money for it anyway.
I'll be grateful for
Mutti's ornate antiques

and all the necessary polishing
I grew up with.
Her furniture will please her.

The Furniture And I

In one place light is refracted
through the bevelled edge on the glass door
like through a diamond;
the polished mahogany shelves
of the vitrine are bare
and the gold filigree key
has a brown label hanging from it.

It's come black market
with the furniture, sent
from Erfurt in the 'Eastern Zone'
to our plain Victorian
terraced house in Leeds.

The vitrine holds a photo of her
standing in the woods with her walking stick.
She's sent the Meissen mocha cups,
a recipe for quince paste,
two silver candlesticks:
Flech, Bolte, Reusch, Günther,
names from Grossvater's regiment,
are engraved around the base.

In the photo
she looks like our neighbour
who seems to get glasspaper
stuck in her throat whenever she speaks.
Does Grossma have some too?

Her tall, dark pieces all stand around
remembering another world and smelling strange;
and the dining-room curtains change to verdigris,
grow little tassles for me to finger.

My mother brings Grossma
down our long front garden path.
Almost bolting up the steps,
Grossma is blocking the light with her black fur coat.

I am standing on the tiled floor.
I hug my ginger cat
tight to my chest

Na! Da ist ja die Kleine!
So this is the little one, she says,
her blue eyes looking into mine
for the first time.

Baking With Grossma

Each year we strolled along the river Main
to the *Weihnachtsmarkt* on the *Römerberg*,
where they sell these Christmas biscuits,
und Bethmännchen, Lebkuchen, Stollen.

I made this dough every Christmas
– up to the war – it's sticky with the butter
so let me roll it out, it has to be thin;
now sprinkle more flour on.

Nun, mein Herzchen, you must choose
your shapes; see, here! There is
the large star, the tiny star, the moon,
the pear and the tree.

And, look! I forgot. The *Buttergebäck*
has also a heart. I sent the cutters from Germany.
We'll paint them with egg yolk to make them shine.
Buttergebäck. Say it, *mein Herzchen*!

Buttergebäck.

Weihnachtsmarkt – Christmas market
Römerberg – Roman Hill, a square in Frankfurt
Bethmännchen, Lebkuchen, Stollen – German Christmas cakes
Nun, mein Herzchen – Now my love, literally 'my little heart'
Buttergebäck – butter biscuits

Headingley & Frankfurt, 1955

Rowing

Through the long sash window the sun
strikes the mahogany table legs;
the adults smoke and talk

and people step out of the black and white photos,
mention where they've come from,

an out-in-the-road sort of place,
and I want to go with them.

Then I'm in an orange crate
with garden canes for the oars;
I row and row
across our long Headingley lawn
day after day
to get me to the Palmengarten

to hear the parrot say,
Babette koch Kaffee,
and discuss how long
that parrot lived for.

Soon I'm standing beside Grossma.
She is asking a German boy,
Kannst du rudern?
Can you row?
Ja.

She pays for him to go
in the boat with me
on the lake in the Palmengarten.
And the oars clunk in the rowlocks
and we glide on the smooth dark surface.

And now Grossma is too far
away to touch, too far to steady
the boat, as we switch seats,
skim the surface of the lake.

And I'm sitting with Grossma
in the rebuilt café,
that serves the *Mohrenköpfe*

learning the taste
my mother tasted as a child,
too creamy rich for me.

And we pass the ruined Opernhaus
with its inscription
Dem Wahren, Schönen, Guten,
'To the True, the Beautiful, the Good';

the Frankfurt adults
from the photos
smoke and talk,

'Weisst du die hat mir das ganze Silber geklaut',
She stole all my silver, that maid, you know.

From Headingley To Chapeltown

Leeds, 1955

It's Sunday, Let's Go To Cowper Street, My father Says

There is fog. And today
Grossma and my mother don't come.

We wait just up the road,
opposite the pillar-box,
by the forty-four bus stop.

My father's hand in its leather glove
holds mine.

The place we get off, on Chapeltown Road,
men in suits and flat caps amble
in and out of the Latvian Club
on the corner.
They dress like Opa Lazar.

Does Opa go the Latvian Club?
No. He goes to the Synagogue.
Can we stop
and buy gherkins at the Polish shop?

Next time. Come on.

Cowper Street, 1955

Oma Leah!

When I stand by the front door a weight
presses down on my shoulders:

the notice in the porch I've made for your tenants,
PLEASE WIPE YOUR FEET ON THE MAT

with a crayoned drawing of a man holding his hat
that looks awkward and doesn't quite work

but you've hung it up anyway, even though
you always tell me Dorothy Burton next door

can do better pictures than me;
the way your shadow

slowly appears through the frosted glass;
how your almost blind eyes

peer through the crack, how the chain
rattles in your shaking hand,

how all your greying hair is brushed
behind your ears and your ear-lobes wobble

with the little diamond earrings;
how every door in the house is locked;

the faded yellowing light in the sitting-room
that falls on the piano where I sit

and get my fingers to do what pianists
do with their fingers, only the sound

mine make is never right.
And how we never come for the Sabbath.

Oma Leah Lectures Me About Miracles

What shall I tell you?
That my great-grandfather
lived to one hundred and six?

That in eleventh century Worms
a carriage
threatened to crush
Rabbi Raschi
in an alleyway
and as he prayed
the wall of the Synagogue
gave way for him?

I am descended from Rabbi Rashi;
my father showed me the stone niche.

He was a gambler, my father,
who played the violin like an angel.

At home in Krakow
he played Wieniawski's
'Souvenir de Moscou',
the light bouncing
off his wavy red hair.

My mother sold his Stradivarius
behind his back;
still my father gambled
till he ruined us.

Rabbi Raschi, (1040–1105): Famed as the author of the first comprehensive commentary on the Talmud

Oma Leah's Wedding Lament

On the day my bankrupt father married me off
the luck sat more in my husband's cup
than mine, believe me. Lazar broke the glass
for us in Krakow; a broken glass
is meant to bring you luck. But I'd already
turned my back on all my dreams, cut up
my ball gown stitched with seed pearls,
the dumb song-birds on my own embroidery;
I spoke sternly to my tiny stubborn heart;
I stood straight with Lazar under the canopy;
I dropped my eyes to his uncultured vowels.
What could I do while the gold band slid
onto my finger? Make a secret vow:
never forgive my father, or fall in love.

Opa Lazar Counts The Cutlery

What were you doing all that time?

I've been counting the cutlery, dear.

I can see you're a good man.

We've got it all, except for the forks.
We're two pieces short, there.

Those are the two I've not polished
but you couldn't know.
Counting the cutlery's right.

We have to watch out for the tenants,
never know what they might be up to.

I can see your intentions are good.

And I've checked all the keys for the doors
and I've put out your robe on your bed.

I can see you're a good man
but I'm going to wash the robe, you know,
and I'm going to strip the beds.

Well, I'll peel you an orange
before you start, and one for me as well.

I'm not hungry right now
but do one for you.

I'm not hungry either now
and not having an orange will be cheaper.

I told you, you were a good man.

Once We Leave Eleven Cowper Street My Father Starts Singing:

Meine Mutter
Schmiert die Butter
Immer an der Wand 'lang,
Immer an der Wand 'lang.

Watch my mother
Spread the butter
All along the wall – oh!
All along the wall – yes!

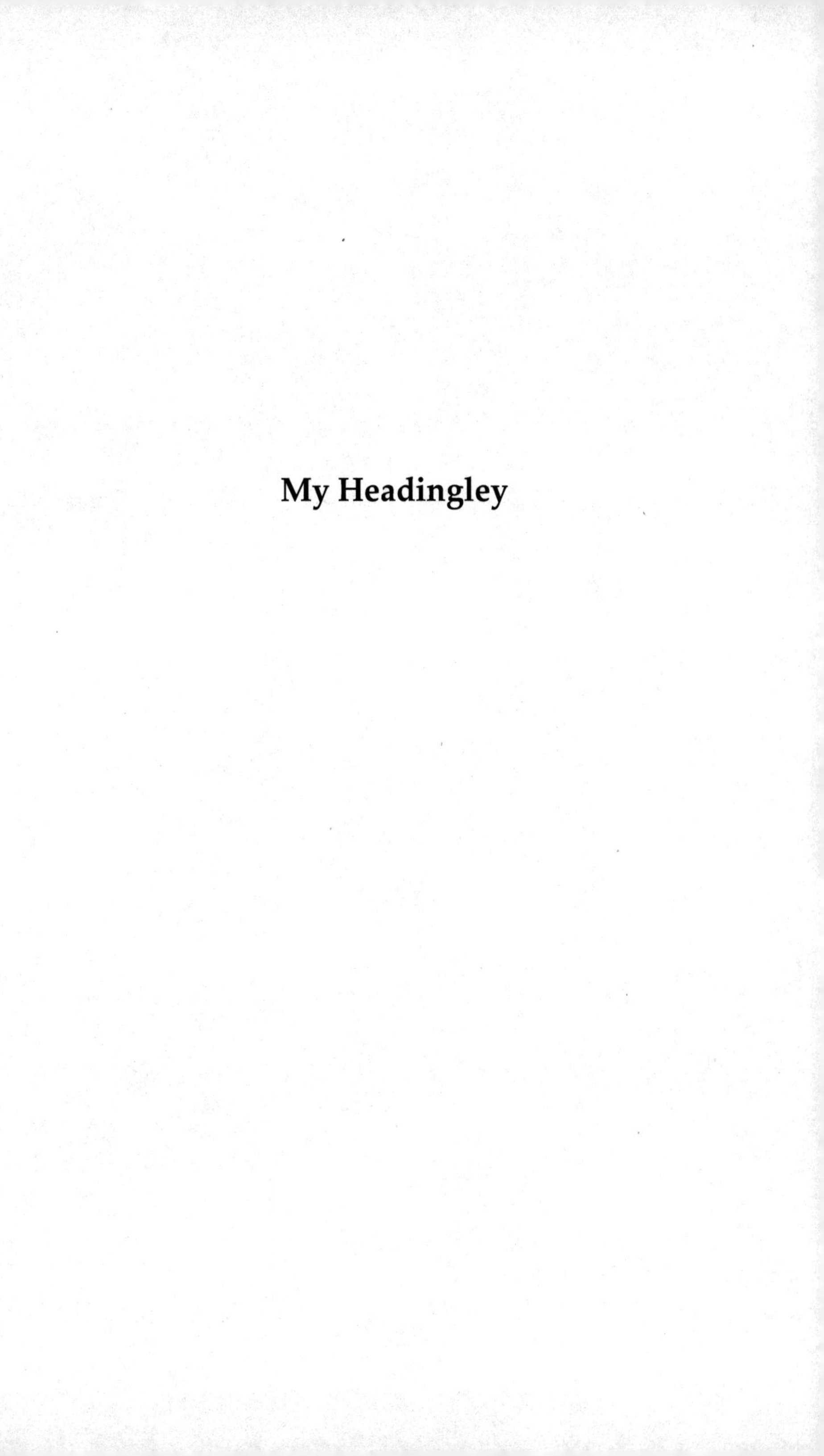

My Headingley

Headingley, 1990

Dear Evelyn,

I couldn't have managed without you,
without the rides I used to have on your back,
the sense of moving forward;
your win on the pools glittered

on your horizon; you were moving towards it
on your kneeling mat, polishing our floor;
it was somewhere in the white skirting boards
or was it in the garden among the forget-me-nots

when we spat on stale bread for luck,
took it to feed the ducks; and you taught me
to pour tea into my saucer to cool,
the times I was late for the bus, then slurp it up?

When I win, you said, I'll buy you
a satin dress, I'll take you to Butlins,
and I knew you would, somewhere
on the fairground where you could play bingo
for a huge shiny doll, or a goldfish,

I'll win you one with ping-pong balls, our lass.

My Father Tells Me...

If you become a doctor like me
you'll be able to work anywhere:
medicine will save you.
We've given you an English name; that will help.
If ever you are widowed,
you'll be able to earn a living.
And if you marry a doctor
then you'll have so much in common
with your husband.

I try to tell him:
I hate science.
He keeps his eyes fixed
firmly on the future.

*

Winter afternoons
I sit and talk to the sky.
I snap a chair-back on take-off,
learn to float through the classroom window,
do breast stroke among clouds;

I think I need help with the touch down.
I catch a cage of birds
who die on landing.
Another time I crash onto the roof of the house
with my dog. He slithers down the slates,
bounces onto the steps;
he leaks blood and guts
onto the stone. You see
not even medicine can save him.

Luckily the physics teacher's teeth
whistle when she speaks.
The only line that hooks me back
is Mrs Taylor describing *spherical surfaces*.

1982

Taking Tea With My Father and Mother

He takes Earl Grey tea
without milk.
It looks like light brown Tizer
in the green glass cup.

The sitting room
is clean and tidy.
It has white walls
a polished Louis Quinze table
Queen Anne bookcase
Biedermeier bureau
floor length, paprika-coloured, velvet curtains
to hide the distant sounds of screaming
coming from the bureau.

Somewhere inside
the second or third drawer down
if he turns the key
and pulls the drawer out
just far enough for it to tip
is an old leather folder with letters.
The tiny brown button inside
keeps the silence.

In the cubicle
the roof is so low
he can't stand up
he can't sit
the seat is so narrow.

Is she still
in the women's cell?

*

A white sky hangs
outside the long sash window.

Sitting opposite him
she eats Danish pastry
sips her tea.

He sits quietly
in his maroon leather slippers.

Recipe No. 7

Torte From Black Bread

1 glass Smetana
1 glass sugar
1 glass black rusks
6 eggs
To bake it all inside the *douchovka*
And to pour over it some rum…

…And...

douchovka – oven

1955 & 1990

Tiddlers

The jam jars carefully tied with string for handles –
the time spent perfecting this tying,
an endless standing by the pantry door –
the tug of the string in my hand
and the jars swinging.

There's the smell of boys
and my oversized rubber soles
slurring on the pavement.
We drink Dandelion and Burdock out of bottles,
taste licorice in sunshine.
We hold the idea of the minnows,
the tiddlers, the light skimming
their scales in the jars.

As we enter the forest
the smell is love-hearts and pear-drops
surrounding us like a fine mist.
We stand in the mud
on the banks of the beck
feeling the excitement of the catch;
we lower our white net.

*

When our daughter was three,
with dark hair at her temples,
and she named her forehead
'my forest'
I did not choose
to remember my own
childhood forest.

*

I've been back now
and I can smell pinks
mixed with overripe pears,
I can see minnows
flicking silver in jam jars.
This time the forest is waist high.

I've netted it now.
I can tell you
it is Himalayan Balsam.

With a name you can know
some of what I mean, as I knew
the tiddlers through glass.

We kept them overnight
in clean water,
and then my father
took me down the road
and I tipped the tiddlers
out of their jam jars,
back into the beck
with the sunlight slicing the water.
I bent over to watch them swim off.

A Few Seats Along

Dorset, September 1988

Todesengel I

My mother is back from holiday.
I am cutting roses for the table;
my mother is beside me.

I dreamt your father
had another woman, she says.

I am cutting the roses for the table.

I can't believe
the pain of it.

The roses are double, pink fading to white.
I am cutting them
from one of the bushes
at the end of the garden.

I had to get up, she says,
and smoke a cigarette
while your father slept.

I am cutting them with the left-handed
scissors with the orange handles,
a bouquet of small thornless roses
that grow in clusters.

I sat there for two hours.

I am cutting the roses from
the other side of the bush.
The soft petals are brushing my skin,
falling through my fingers.

Todesengel – Angel of Death

Todesengel II

(Telling My Husband The Dream)

And I come up the brick steps from the garden
into the kitchen with the roses
to find my husband:

My mother dreamt
my father had another woman.

Now he's taken his second retirement,
he says, she's rehearsing
for the day when he dies.

Headingley & Dorset, October 1988

A Phone Call From My Mother

Hello. It's about your father:
he said this morning,
I'll go and get my gardening clothes
I'll go into the garden,
he seemed leisurely for him;
it's our first day back from our trip,
his first day of retirement –
he'd be back at work normally by ten;
he was a long time getting changed;
I went upstairs to the bedroom
and he was sitting there
in the corner, on the chair
beside the wardrobe,
in his grey gardening trousers and grey shirt
ready to go.

Hello, I said.
I've had a stroke, he said.

(You're forgetting
the angel of death, the *Todesengel*!
the woman in your dream.)

It's ten o'clock,
he said,
I would just have started work.

*

I got him to bed
and his eyes began to roll in his head:
Good-bye, Lottie. I love you.
Good-bye Kurt…

I'm only half now

Dorset, 1988

Holding On

I have a map of my garden
drawn in ink by the previous owner
with the rose bush on it.
I keep trying to identify it:
pink flowers fading to white,
a small thornless rose
that grows in clusters.
Even in catalogues
I can't find its name.

Headingley, 1988

The Taste That Is Left Behind

All the way in the train I cry.
And I read my book.
All the way from the station
the rain falls on his city.

I stand on the tarmac garden path
with my mother at the top
of the stone steps, opening
the front door.
I walk through the door.

In the empty bathroom I wash
my hands and smell his soap,
Cussons Imperial Leather.

*

My mother serves me Danish pastry.
The taste that is left behind –
a bitter, metallic taste on my tongue.

*

At night my dreams let rats
loose on the kitchen floor,
let rats crouch in the roasting pan.
Come quick ! I'm out – by the back door!

*

In the day he whispers to me,
Come home!
Yes, I say. I've come
to bring you lily of the valley
from your garden:
I've come to say good-bye.

August 1990

My Mother Talks To My Father's Photo On The Escritoire

Dusk is falling and the house is quiet.
Downstairs our green dining room smells of fresh polish.
Remember when my mother
sent us the furniture from Erfurt, Kurt:
the onyx table and candlesticks,
the sideboard with the marble top.

In the kitchen the instruction booklets are laid out,
one on the dishwasher,
the other on the washing machine;
I've stocked the freezer with food, for when Pam comes up;
the cooking instructions for the chicken
are in the letter to her,
I've left it on the table;
I've hung clean towels on the rail
at the back of the partition, next to the sink;
and put a new Brillo pad
into the red frog holder on the window sill.

Look through the window and you can see
my little kitchen garden is full of flowers.
For the first time the yucca has great, cream blooms.

I've chosen this little back bedroom.
I hope the eight Tuinol tablets you got
from the chemists eight years ago, Kurt,
haven't lost their strength.
You thought you would be the one to use them
but, annoyingly, you went first.
They were easier to swallow than I thought,
so I hope I won't wake with a dry mouth.

I've got six green tumblers, full of water,
on the walnut table beside me –
just in case.

They say when you die
the whole of your life flashes before you.
There is so much I've tried to forget…

And the hardest thing is to say good-bye to Pam.
She's been a good daughter.
But I need my rest.

Kurt. It's going to be alright.
It wasn't really good-bye when you died

And I'm Clearing Up The House...

Now you're gone, mother,
I wear your pink angora cardigan.
I like its softness against my neck and wrists,
your smell of cigarettes and Joy de Patou.

I find it edgy in the house without you.
You've put everything in order for me,
even tied the right key to each suitcase
in the attic. You would!

*

You know that Russian proverb?
It's in Solzhenitsyn:
'No. Don't! Don't dig up the past.
Dwell on the past and you lose an eye.'

It goes on:
'Forget the past
and you'll lose two eyes.'

en route, 1995

I Realise

My angels will always speak in German
faintly, so I can't quite catch their meaning,
just the sound; they disguise themselves
as grey-haired old ladies, sitting around
on the platform a certain distance away from me.
I don't know if they board the train with me
or just are there again, a few seats along;
I get closer on my way to the buffet
and they lose their music,
become students, speak in English.

It's a blessing they're so able to outwit me,
hint at where they come from now and then,
as if they know I never wanted to be German
except on Christmas Eve to light the candles on the tree.

Krakow, 1995

Uncle Marek

I found an envelope,
a white one
with writing in blue ink:
Dr Marek Margulies
Krakow
U Pilsudskiego 36/37
– torn open.

What was it like
in the sunshine
in the best days?

What was it like in Krakow, uncle Marek?
Did you eat at the Kurza Stopska?
Did you eat clear red borshch
with boiled eggs floating in it
in the white and oak panelled room,
before the Nazis?

Uncle Marek, you
looked after my father
on his way to Russia,
you looked after my mother,
you gave their mixed marriage
your unmixed blessing.

I've seen the balcony,
the mosaic over the door
to your house
in the street near the university.

That's where you'd have read,
on a triangle of lavatory paper,
my father's tiny pencilled message,
smuggled from Kiev
in the white envelope.

'Dear uncle Marek,
Lottie und ich sind im August verhaftet
Lottie and I were arrested in August.
Please let my parents know.
We hope to get out soon.
Um uns mach Dir keine Sorgen
Don't worry about us.'

It has brought me here
to the stone lion at the bottom of the tower
in the yellowed September sunshine
on the square of the Rynek Glowny;
I'm sure I can hear your voice
beside my right shoulder, uncle Marek;
you're not speaking German, or Polish or Yiddish:
I suppose it's an intonation, the song of it,
a quiet, deep timbre
with a hint of a rasp in your throat;
you know how on a warm summer evening
when the temperature drops,
there's condensation in the air
and from across the valley
suddenly you can hear the river.

Chronology

1905 Leah & Lazar marry in Krakow

1907 Kurt born in Frankfurt/Main

1911 Lottie born in Frankfurt/Main

1914-18 First World War

1933 Kurt & Lottie's courtship begins

1933 Hitler comes to power in Germany. Hermann Göring appointed Cabinet Minister Without Portfolio

1934 Kurt loses his job, along with many Jewish doctors, teachers, lawyers, journalists. He begins working in the Hospital of Jewish Congregation

1934 Hermann Göring arranges the Night of the Long Knives

1934-5 Kurt & Lottie elope to Kharkov, Ukraine, USSR where they begin work at the Metschnikov Institute

1935 Nuremberg Laws deprive Jews of German citizenship & forbid them to marry non Jews. Hermann Göring becomes Chief of the Air force

1935 Kurt & Lottie marry in Kharkov

1937 One of the worst Stalin Purges. At its height in August Kurt & Lottie arrested & sent to Kiev due to prison overcrowding

1938 (May) Kurt & Lottie released from Kiev prison & deported. They make their way to England via Poland

1938 (August) Kurt becomes research assistant to Prof JW McLeod, Leeds Medical School

1938 (November) Kristallnacht

1939 (April) Leah & Lazar come to England

1939 (September) World War 2 declared

194? Grossma Hertha & Grossvater Erich move to Erfuhrt

1940 Internment of Germans and Austrians living in Great Britain, irrespective of whether they are Jewish, or Nazi. Most are interned on the Isle of Man, including Kurt & Lottie & Lazar

1940 (November) Lazar released from the Isle of Man on his 65th birthday

1941 Kurt & Lottie released from the Isle of Man

194? Uncle Marek dies in Auschwitz

1945 World War 2 ends

1945 Pam is born

1945-6 The Soviet Union annexes East Germany and the border dividing East and West Germany is drawn, Cold War begins

1947 Grossvater Erich dies in East Germany

1949 East Germany becomes the German Democratic Republic

1950 Grossma Hertha escapes from the German Democratic Republic & arrives in Leeds via Frankfurt

1955 Grossma Hertha & Pam visit Frankfurt

(1959 Opa Lazar dies)

(1967 Oma Leah dies)

1974 Pam marries Peter Hope

(1976 Grossma Hertha dies)

1988 Kurt dies

1989 Communist rule overthrown in Poland

1990 Fall of the Berlin Wall

1990 Lottie dies

1995 Pam visits Krakow

Sources

Before she died, my mother assembled an extensive archive which has been a helpful source of inspiration and information for several of the poems as my parents rarely spoke of their experiences.

During the 1990s I interviewed three of my mother's surviving friends: Mathilde Goldschmidt and Elizabeth May, both now deceased, and Erna Schütz. I am indebted to all of them for valuable insights and information.

The cigarette papers are in the archive, in an envelope marked 'Russische Kochrezepte. Nicht wegwerfen' (Russian recipes, don't throw away). The recipes have been translated by Ellen Kaminsky, a few by Sandy Lukiannchikova and by the late Sonya Goldsmith. I am indebted to them all for the trouble they took.

'Der Magistrat – Personaldezernent' is a version of the translation of a document (in the form of photocopies) in the archive.

Knowledge of Grossvater Erich's phone call to Göring comes from conversations with Mathilde Goldschmidt, without whose help this book would probably not have been written.

The brochure and postcard with details of the Putyovka are edited and reworked from a talk my father gave at Leeds University, during the War. His m/s for it is in the archive.

'Erna's Tale' arose out of Erna Schütz's description of this incident in her autobiography.

The story of the message written on the cubicle door was told by my mother to a neighbour shortly before she died.

Franz Gugenheim was my father's best friend. He came to England in 1935 as one of fifty immigrant Jewish GPs allowed to practice here. He and his wife took Kurt and Lottie into their home in 1938 when they first arrived in England.

'Letters', between my father and my mother on the Isle of Man, are edited and reworked from originals in the archive.

'The Ballad of the German Refugee' is in the archive. The music is by Hans Gal, lyrics by Richard Hutter, et al.

'To The Housefather, House Number 6' is an edited version of the original document in the archive.

The letter Grossvater Erich wrote to my mother (in German) is in the archive. 'It's been thirteen years since I heard from you' is the only quote, though he does mention his cough.

The poem 'Grossma Writes' is an edited and reworked version of a letter I found in the archive. The original letter is far longer, written over several days, without paragraphs, to save paper and stamps.

The tiny brown button is in the archive.

The message on lavatory paper described in 'Uncle Marek' is in the archive, accompanied by a letter to Uncle Marek from Sternberg, the man who smuggled the message out of gaol, wrote the address on the white envelope and posted the letter. My father's message also asks Uncle Marek to help this colleague Sternberg as much as he can. In the event I doubt that Sternberg and uncle Marek met.

Literary Sources

Stalin Purges

Borderland: A Journey Through the History of Ukraine
by Anna Reid
The Great Terror: A Reassessment by Robert Conquest
Die Gross Lüge by Erna Schütz
The Gulag Archipelago by Alexander Sozhenitsyn
Night of Stone: Death and Memory in Russia
by Catherine Merridale
Requiem: Poems 1935-40 by Anna Akhmatova
Till My Tale is Told: Women's Memoirs of the Gulag
edited by Simeon Vilensky

Isle of Man

Internment on the Isle of Man by Connery Chappell
Island of Barbed Wire: The Remarkable Story of World War Two

General

Art and Power – Europe under the dictators, 1930-45
(Catalogue to Hayward Gallery Exhibition)

Second Generation Survivors

Children of the Holocaust by Helen Epstein
Lost in Translation: A Life in a New Language by Eva Hoffman

Acknowledgements

Poems from *On Cigarette Papers* have been published in the following anthologies: *Stripe,* Templar 2009; *New Writing 15,* edited by Bernardine Evaristo and Maggie Gee, British Council/Granta 2007; *Parents,* Enitharmon 2000; *Images of Women,* Arrowhead 2006; and in the following magazines: *European Judaism, Poetry London, Stand, Staple, Dream Catcher.*